FACEBOOK PORTAL

USER GUIDE

User manual for Facebook Portal TV | Portal Plus | Portal Go | Portal Mini

Contents

Introduction

The Facebook Portal device is a smart display launched by Facebook, now known as Meta. The Portal comes with built-in Alexa smart assistance, and its main function is to make video calls, access Facebook, WhatsApp, and Instagram. You need to own one of the mentioned accounts to use the Portal. Aside the video call thing, the device doesn't just sit there when you're not making a call. It has a few other features you are likely to find amazing, like its AR effects, storytelling and did I mention it serves as an amazing digital photo frame. It's somewhat an Alexa device with a screen (a very large one), and a camera that could move.

Currently, the Portal device comes in four different designs, which offer mostly the same experience with similar features and slight differences in specifications.

There's the Portal TV (which doesn't have a screen at all), the premium 14-inch Portal Plus, the larger 10-inch Portal (which was upgraded to Portal Go with an in-built battery), and the small but snazzy 8-inch Portal Mini.

Each is designed to slot comfortably into your home, and give you the premium video call experience with friends and family members even while you're on the move.

Since all the different variants mostly offer a very similar experience and functionality, your choice should now be greatly influenced by how much screen real estate you want and your budget.

Features you may find interesting

➢ **Versatile Augmented Reality:** Portal is equipped with ever-improving animation and AR effects, creating an almost real-life experience with every feature and more.
The AR can add masks to calls, turn your background to some location from fairy tales, and add a cinema-like experience to story times.

➢ **Story Time for your kids:** Facebook updates Story Time with new children's books from time to time. Story Time is a mode that uses face detection to apply filters and masks, to bring more life into the story. It gives masks and effects to match every stage of read-alongs of popular kid stories as you go. Granted, it may be a little weird to use your Portal as a bedtime storybook, but you'll definitely love the color it paints of your story. This feature can also come in with video calls from a distance, which makes it fun for parents on trips who want to interact with their kids.

➤ **Bluetooth connectivity:** You can link your Portal with any other Bluetooth-enabled device. Like smartphones, headphones, and even keyboards.

➤ **Distant watching with friends using Portal TV:** Part of the appeal of Facebook Portal is staying social — even if you're just watching TV. With a Portal TV, you can watch videos with friends from a distance. This extra feature is a unique perk with Portal, and there's nothing else like it (yet). You can link up to seven people with the "Watch Together" feature and view any of Facebook's Watch video content while running a live stream on the side. Start by making a video call with a friend or friends, then use the Facebook Watch TV menu to launch a show. Your live stream with friends will be in a square in the corner of your TV, and Portal will make sure the video remains synced for both of you.

➢ **Superframe:** This is simply the photo slideshow your Portal displays when not being actively used. The smart screen itself controls this feature to cycle through the most recent photos you've shared on Facebook, but this feature also has a lot of customization options users should take a look at. It can also show when your preselected contacts are available to connect with.

Under settings, you can find options to set the cycle speed of photos (10 or 15 seconds) and, more importantly, where your photos are coming from. This allows you to choose photos from a specific online album, your own Facebook profile, only photos that you're tagged in, or photos from the friends who are tagged as one of your favorites on Portal. This should be one of the first things you set.

➢ **Adjust privacy features:** Some users may never get very comfortable with living with an eye looking at them all day in their homes. There are some privacy features made just to ease you of the bother. Right at the top of your Portal, there is a single privacy switch that can slide to shut off the microphone and camera on the device. A small red light by the screen that indicates when these features are turned off (if the light isn't on, the mic and camera are). These buttons are always there but may vary a little depending on what

Portal device you have. Portals also come with a cover that you can use to physically cover up the camera if it's particularly annoying to you (but this doesn't in any way shut off the microphone). Try out these features and use them according to your privacy needs.

➤ **Amazon Alexa Built-In:** Portal has a compromise: It uses Alexa for its voice commands. If you have used an Echo device, you may be familiar with how Alexa works, but those new to the voice assistant should put some time into learning how it works. You may want to get our Alexa user guide (see the end of this book) if you don't have an idea how this AI works. Alexa can connect with many, many smart devices that you may have around your home and control them. You can browse through many Alexa skills and enable specific data skills that you want to use.

It's also important to bear in mind that you won't be able to use any Alexa skill that requires a display to work, because Alexa doesn't have a display presence on the Portal device. That means you won't be having anything like the Echo Show user experience, like adjusting your home lighting via a touchscreen.

➤ **The camera moves:** The Portal's camera moves around to follow people in a room, which is amazing, and nice for having frequent video conversations with the liberty to move about the room when on call. Multiple people milling around in the room might confuse the camera. Tap on your face twice when you are talking and a square will surround your face, so Portal will know to always follow you.

➢ **Compatible with some favorite apps:** The Portal device continues to get app compatibility that allows you to use various apps directly from the Portal interface. Users should keep up with the latest apps so they know what they can use via Portal. Here's a quick list of some of Portal's popular apps:

- Amazon Prime Video, Showtime, and other streaming services
- News stations like CNN and ABC
- Food Network
- Spotify and Pandora
- Quick links to popular sites like Google, Amazon, YouTube, Reddit, NPR, and AllRecipes for browsing online right from the Portal
- Watch, which is key to playing games on your Portal and a good download for everyone

You can easily search and download apps onto your Portal at any time, by going to the Home section and selecting Apps.

➤ **Customize calling and notifications zone:** Facebook Portal has a Home and Away function which can be used to tell your device how, and where you want to make calls or get alerts. Sweep left from the home screen, and tap on Settings > Incoming Call Settings. You may prefer to switch on "Only When You're Home". This will set the Portal to allow incoming calls only when it senses you are around, otherwise a Facebook call will be directed to your smartphone. Confirm on your phone, and you're good to go.

There's a complementary system that works well with this: Find the people you like talking to on Facebook when you are using Portal, select their name, and tap the "i" icon in the window that pops up about them. Then Portal will give you an alert and make a small sound whenever they are actively using Facebook, which means they're probably in a good position to take video calls.

Remember, you don't need a Portal device to make video calls with Messenger or WhatsApp app on your phone.

➤ **"Hey Portal" commands:** Portal has its own voice assistant in addition to Alexa, which you can activate by saying, "Hey, Portal." It's fairly limited, but you can use it to control any of Portal's major functions. That includes "Hey Portal, call [contact name]" or "Hey Portal, lower brightness." You can also say, "Hey Portal, good morning," to get a report on the weather, news, scheduled events, and birthdays. Be mindful that Facebook does keep and may even examine Hey Portal recordings.

➢ **Browse the web more easily:** While the function isn't exactly seamless, Portal does allow you to search the web with a basic browser. The touch controls get old fast, though. Fortunately, Portal does have Bluetooth compatibility that extends to mice and keyboards. Get an affordable Bluetooth mouse and a keyboard to go with it, and browsing becomes far easier. Adding a couple of accessories allows you to turn your Portal into a central house computer that anyone can hop on when they need to.

➢ **Setting up a passcode:** Privacy and security are paramount for any data housing service, and Portal is no exception. It's crucial to set up a passcode to keep outsiders from accessing your account. You can easily set up a four-digit code by opening Settings, then Passcode. Portal will then time out and ask you to unlock it with the four-digit code. You'll also need to enter your passcode when you change other account settings.

How to set up your Facebook Portal

How to set up the Facebook Portal so you can take full advantage of its numerous features, plus video calls using Messenger and WhatsApp.

The Facebook Portal smart display is great at making video calls to Facebook Messenger and WhatsApp contacts. The setup process can be quite straightforward, but it's somewhat lengthy. In case the Portal's instructions are confusing to you, here is a step-by-step guide to set up the Facebook Portal.

1. Unbox the Facebook Portal.

2. Plug the power cord into the charging port at the back of the Portal, and plug the other end into an outlet.

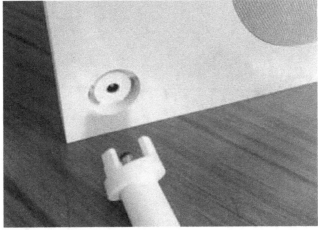

3. The Portal boots up and prompts you to select your language.

4. Connect to your Wi-Fi network.

5. Once the Portal connects to the internet, it will automatically download and install the latest update. During this time, you can take a virtual tour of the device.

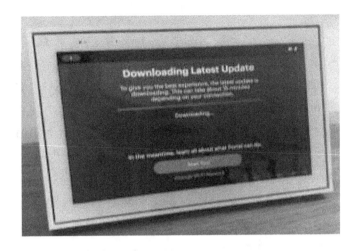

6. After the Portal has finished updating, it will prompt you to restart it.

7. After the restart, press "continue" to accept the terms of service.

8. Choose a name for your Portal. You can create your own name, or select from the menu.

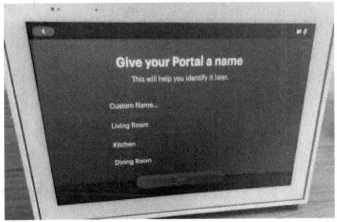

9. Add your Facebook account. You can enter your Facebook password directly on the Portal itself, or alternatively, a code will appear on the screen of the Portal. Then use the web browser on your computer or smartphone, visit www.facebook.com/device and enter the code to connect to your Facebook account. If you successfully connect your account, a screen should appear confirming this. Press Next to continue.

10. Connect your WhatsApp account (optional). If you opt to connect your WhatsApp account to the Portal, a QR code will appear on the Portal's display. Open the WhatsApp account on your smartphone; on iPhones, go to Settings, and on Android phones, go to chats and select the three vertical dots. Next, select WhatsApp Web, and hold your smartphone's camera up so that it can read the QR code.

11. Select your favorite contacts. These are the profiles that will always be visible, so you can more easily call them from the Portal.

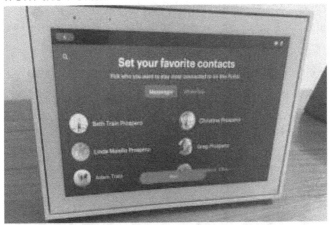

12. Choose to hide contacts (optional). If you don't want all of your contacts to appear on the Portal, you can hide them, if you so choose.

13. Next, you can see how the Portal's camera works; it can lock on to your face, and digitally zoom and pan to keep you in the frame as you walk around the room. You can skip this step if you want.

14. Connect Pandora and Spotify. If you have accounts with either of these music streaming services, you can link them to the Portal. Select "connect" next to the service you wish to use.

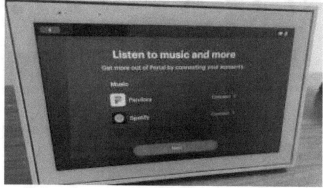

15. If you want to use the Portal as a digital picture frame, select Preview Facebook Photos, and then Add Facebook Photos on the next screen. You can choose which Facebook albums you want to display. Later, you can also connect your Instagram account if you want to display photos from there, too.

16. Select Get Portal App if you want to add photos directly from your phone. This will require you to install a separate app on your smartphone.

17. Connect Alexa if you have an Alexa account, and want to use it on the Portal. We recommend using Alexa rather than the Portal's own voice assistant, as Amazon's assistant is far more capable.

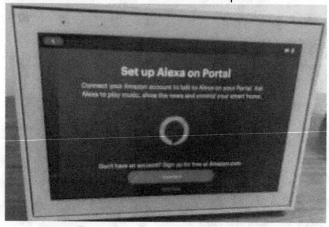

18. Press Next to use the "Hey Portal" trigger to initiate video calls.

19. The last step is to allow the Portal to store your "Hey Portal" voice recordings so that Facebook can listen to them in order to improve its voice-recognition capabilities. This is optional, and even if you agree to this during the setup process, you can turn this off and delete all your recordings at a later time.

20. Your Facebook Portal should be set up now. The main home screen should display your favorite contacts as well as those individuals whom you called recently. If you swipe to the left, you'll see all of your installed apps, Contacts, and Settings.

18

Facebook Portal and Your Privacy

Should You Trust Facebook Portal with Your Privacy?

It's not that we have trust issues, but we're very nervous about Facebook's security scandals, but the company has assured users that the Portal is designed with their privacy in mind. It's not perfect, of course. You've should be wary of "false wakes", where the unit starts recorded when it thinks you've said "Hey Portal".

What Information Does Facebook Portal Collect?

Read that sentence again. Because yes, Facebook nonetheless does collect some of your information. This primarily relates to things you say to your Portal.

Facebook Portal records and transcribes what say to it, once it hears "Hey Portal". This information plus the background noise is then sent to Facebook's servers. Facebook eventually deletes this. Though it can take three years.

However, you need to turn your microphone off. It means the device won't respond to "Hey Portal". This will prevent "false wakes" and other things that follow it.

So, does Facebook Portal store any information related to your video calls? Yes. It does. Though your actual video contents are kept private, technical details are relayed to

Facebook. The company says this includes "volume level, frame resolution, number of bytes received".

A crash report is another form of data that is logged on your Portal and sent to Facebook. This set of data usually reveals how many people that were in the frame when the Portal stopped working and their distances from the microphones.

This is suggestive of more information sent to Facebook. To perfect the performance feedback, it'll also collate data about ambient light, system logs, and settings.

Now, that's about your video calls. But what about third-party apps? The Portal has an in-built browser and a limited app store; some apps are pre-loaded too. And yes, these open more questions about privacy. Facebook communicates with third parties.

Sometimes, this is just about app usage: frequency, bugs, and length of time you use them. Sometimes, more information is mined. To find out more, you have to check out the independent privacy policies of each app. It takes time, but it's worth finding out exactly what personal details you're surrendering.

How Is Collected Information Used?

Facebook maintains that most of the data collected are for performance reasons only. Information develops the AIs, so, for instance, results to "Hey Portal" inquiries are accurate. These are reviewed by actual people, not merely a computer.

These Facebook workers are monitored so they comply with privacy and security strictures.

But your voice commands can be shared with third parties. Recordings and transcripts are sent to service providers like Alexa once more to improve the service. Transcripts are shared with apps for accuracy in response to "Hey Portal" inquiries.

An added caveat is in your favor: the pitch of your voice is altered so no one can personally identify you that way.

However, further identifiers are shared, like your Portal's name, IP address, and zip code.

How Can You Protect Your Information?

If you select another language, voice commands are disabled. "Hey Portal" is only available in English at the time of launch. This will greatly reduce how useful your device is, though.

Thanks to the General Data Protection Regulation (GDPR). There are actions you can take to protect your data. You can access and delete your recordings, meaning Facebook won't store any voice commands.

You can disable storage completely in your Portal Settings, so you can still use "Hey Portal" but it won't log what you say. The downside is that it won't be as fast or as accurate as devices that store data, although it's doubtful you'll even notice this lag.

Another thing is that the company can tell what times you use Portal and how often, because system usage is still logged.

To alter this, you'll need to sign into Facebook, navigate to your profile, then click on Activity Log. This is a list of every time you've signed into Portal or Facebook, plus all your reacts and comments. You can delete accordingly. You may want to be careful there if you're not familiar with that kind of stuff.

Currently, there is no simple way to stop the company from sharing device information like IP addresses.

Could Facebook Portal be spying on you?

A camera permanently at a vantage in your living room should immediately raise concerns. So, too, should its microphone, which some think may be used to eavesdrop on everything sound you make.

After all, worries about smart devices spying on their owners persist. Just examine those reports of targeted ads apparently drawn from discussions had with family and friends.

Users are now naturally skeptical of Facebook's intentions, but millions still use it every day. Still, you can control the level of information you put online. The main potential issue with Facebook Portal is that you don't know what data is collected and who can access that which has been collected.

Can Facebook Portal Identify Faces?

You must be familiar with how facial recognition works. Tags are suggested when you add photos of family and friends on Facebook. The company's Deep Face technology will then be used to build an artificial map of the faces in the pictures. Naturally, you ought to be wondering, does Facebook Portal use facial recognition software? Does it know who's talking?

Fortunately, not. The AI is used to track motion, so the camera can pan across a room. The Portal doesn't recognize your face. It isn't there for malicious intent. Nonetheless, it has the capability to lock onto faces, so the Portal automatically zooms and still keeps you in shot during a video call session. It's also used when activating AR.

This AI runs locally, meaning on your actual Portal, not on Facebook's servers.

Does the Portal's Microphone Listen All the Time?

You can disable the microphone, as we previously mentioned. Know that you'll have to physically turn it back on again before it'll listen to voice commands again. If you only covered the lens with the shutter, your mic stays on and so it can still react when you say "Hey Portal".

But no system is infallible, so Facebook subtly warns about "false wakes", i.e. when you say something else and the device wrongly identifies something you say as "Hey Portal". Such interpretation error is deleted within 90 days.

Troubleshooting your Facebook Portal

Portal trips, reboots unexpectedly, or just won't turn on: Here are a few things you can try: Check if the power button is stuck. Plug your portal into a different power source. Unplug anything attached to your Portal (including extension cord). If the problem persists, then do a factory reset.

Portal TV unexpectedly switches your TV on and off: Try unplugging all other devices from your TV except for your Portal TV. If your Portal TV is working as expected, plug the other devices back in, one at a time.

Touch screen not working as it should: Check accessibility options. It might have been mistakenly turned on during setup.

Poor video quality on Portal: Weak signal is the common cause of blurry, pixelated, or freezing video call experience.

Audio issues or echo on Portal TV: Make sure your TV is set to the right input, and volume not too high.

Can't find your contacts on Portal: If you can't find a contact on Portal, make sure you're signed in with the right account. Additionally, check hidden contacts or restart your Portal.

Error message while trying to make a call on Portal: check for software update, if you receive error messages when you try to make a call on Portal. It might be a sign your Portal is running an old version of the Portal software.

Portal doesn't ring when I call from the Messenger app: If a Portal doesn't ring after an attempted call, you may be on a version of Messenger that is incompatible with Portal.

Can't pair your Portal with a new Portal TV remote: To pair your new remote, you'll have to factory reset your Portal TV.

Calls dropping automatically on Porta: Check the signal strength at both ends of the call. Weak signal is the most common cause of calls dropping in the middle of your conversation.

Get the updated Alexa hack handbook: useful and fun tips, tricks, and features that are not commonly known.

ASIN: B08RT7K5CB

www.ingramcontent.com/pod-product-compliance
Lightning Source LLC
LaVergne TN
LVHW051752050326
832903LV00029B/2874